THE TREE THAT HOLDS UP THE SKY

Paul King

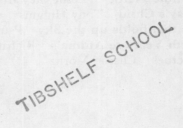

The right of the University of Cambridge to print and sell all manner of books was granted by Henry VIII in 1534. The University has printed and published continuously since 1584.

Cambridge University Press

CAMBRIDGE

NEW YORK   NEW ROCHELLE

MELBOURNE   SYDNEY

ACT NOW PLAYS

Series editor: Peter Rowlands
Founding editor: Andrew Bethell

Roots, Rules and Tribulations   Andrew Bethell
Closed Circuit   Mike English
Faust and Furious   Anne Lee
Czechmate   Gerry Docherty and Bill Kinross
Spring Offensive   Ray Speakman and Derek Nicholls
Football Apprentices   David Holman
Gregory's Girl   Bill Forsyth
Vacuees   Bill Martin
Easy on the Relish   Andrew Bethell
Fans   Mike English
Three Minute Heroes   Leslie Stewart
Wednesday's Child   Tony Higgins
The Tree that holds up the Sky   Paul King
The Fourth Year are Animals   Richard Tulloch
Fit for Heroes   Charlie Moritz

Published by the Press Syndicate of the University of Cambridge
The Pitt Building, Trumpington Street, Cambridge CB2 1RP
32 East 57th Street, New York, NY 10022, USA
10 Stamford Road, Oakleigh, Melbourne 3166, Australia

© Cambridge University Press 1987

First published 1987

Printed in Great Britain by
David Green Printers Ltd, Kettering, Northamptonshire

GR

ISBN 0 521 34997 4

Performance
For permission to give a public performance of *The Tree that holds up the Sky* please write to Permissions Department, Cambridge University Press, The Edinburgh Building, Shaftesbury Road, Cambridge CB2 2RU.

ABOUT THE PLAY

A community of people are living in the heart of the tropical rain forest, untouched by 'civilisation'. Their beliefs centre on the sacred Tree, whose branches hold up the sky. When surveyors arrive from the outside world with plans to build a motorway through the forest, village peace is shattered and the community is bitterly divided.

The Tree that holds up the Sky is based on a genuine belief. There are tribes in the Amazon basin who believe that the sky is held up by a huge forked stick. I heard this on the radio a few years ago and it stuck in my mind. I filed it away as being an interesting subject on which to base a play. I wanted to write about the way we view and treat people of cultures that are different from our own. We are often too keen to dismiss other people's beliefs because we usually think we are right. I also wanted to write a play which in some way dealt with issues of pollution, conservation and the bomb and it seemed a good vehicle with which to do it.

The Tree that holds up the Sky, first performed by the Hampshire County Youth Theatre in 1985, was originally conceived as a musical, and has now been specially adapted for the *Act Now* series.

Paul King

CHARACTERS

In order of appearance

The People

ASPEN (F) A mystical and strange figure who stands aloof from the action

JUNIPER (F)
HYACINTH (F)
ALTHEA (F)
AMARYLLIS (F)
} THE CHORUS: they provide comment on the action. They have an air of knowing more than they are prepared to tell. They are often cynical and sneering

POPPY (F) Lively and energetic – someone who will give everything for a cause

MARIGOLD (F) A steady character who will usually do the right thing without quite knowing why

TANSY (F) Impatient and outgoing – someone who will take risks and who is prepared to meet the future head on

ALLYSSUM (F) A dreamer who looks to the future

PRIMROSE (F) Sharp, bright and intelligent

ALDER (M) A steady and stalwart upholder of the old order

SORREL (M) Outgoing, fun-loving and lively

COLUMBINE (F) Very much an individual who is prepared to please herself and nobody else

MOSS (M) A hot-headed character with a short fuse, and upholder of the old order

BRYONY (F) Outgoing, intelligent and firm. She can be ruthless when necessary. Also an upholder of the old order

BRACT (M) Forceful and a natural leader

HOLLY (F) Outward looking, bright-eyed, curious and enthusiastic

ASH (M) Holly's boyfriend. He is pleasant and easily contented until roused into action

CLEOME (F) The leader of the people. She is a calm character who will try to see both sides of any argument

The Crew

FORD (M) Intelligent, cynical and pushy. He makes fun of everyone and everything, including himself

MORRIS (M) Ford's friend. He is often worried and has a kind of nervous humour. He can be perceptive

AUSTIN (M) The foreman. He will usually get the job done without asking too many questions unless it really goes against the grain

BENTLEY (M) An enthusiast for technology

RILEY (M) A romantic

ALLARD (F) The boss. She is a self-made woman who is used to getting things done and to having her own way

SCOTT (F) The company anthropologist. She works for the company but is sympathetic towards the people. In an ideal world she would like the best for everybody

---

STAGE DIRECTIONS

There are two kinds of directions in this playscript. Those in **bold type** provide information that is essential to an understanding of what is happening in the play at that time. For a play-reading, these should be read by a separate reader.

Those in *italic type* are less essential stage directions and offer suggestions to assist with a production of the play on stage. In a reading they are best not read out as they will hamper the flow of the play, although those who are reading may find that some of these instructions offer help with the interpretation of their lines.

ACT ONE

SCENE 1   **A large clearing in a tropical forest; in the middle there is a tall tree. There is dense undergrowth all around but a number of paths lead into the clearing.**

ASPEN **walks slowly into the clearing – she is a magical and mysterious figure. She stands and slowly surveys the audience. After a moment's silence she begins to speak.**

ASPEN   Once there was a primeval forest that stretched out forever and beyond. In the middle of the forest was a clearing; in the clearing was a village, and in the village lived the people.

(THE PEOPLE **enter. They come quietly in through all the entrances and they take their places in the clearing.** *JUNIPER*, *HYACINTH*, *AMARYLLIS* **and** *ALTHEA* **who are the** CHORUS **move to a high position so that they are looking down on the others.**)

ASPEN   In the beginning was darkness. The sky lay upon the ground in mist and in shadow. The forest could not grow, the animals were denied life and the people were shut out from the light of the day. The Creator of All Things was saddened by what he saw so he took it upon himself to sow a seed. That seed became a tree, a tree which grew strong and tall. As it grew it pushed up the sky and made a space for all things to live. And the Creator said to the people, 'You are the Guardians of the Tree. Keep it well for it holds up the sky.'

(Everyone except the Chorus stands very still looking at Aspen.)

JUNIPER   Today is Treeday!

HYACINTH   The most wonderful day of the year.

ALTHEA	The highlight of the calendar.
AMARYLLIS	Happy Treeday!
THE PEOPLE	Happy Treeday! *(Everyone smiles and looks happy.)*
JUNIPER	Have a terrific Treeday.
ALTHEA	Have a tumultuous Treeday.

(**All the people are carrying bright and glittering decorations. They begin to decorate the clearing and the Tree. All the time** ASPEN **and the** CHORUS **are watching.**)

JUNIPER	The village burbles with activity.
HYACINTH	People scurry hither and thither.
ALTHEA	Things to do – preparations to make.
AMARYLLIS	With joy in their hearts and a spring in their step they adorn the Tree. They decorate the glade.

(**MARIGOLD is busy putting decorations on the Tree. POPPY is standing watching her.**)

POPPY	That's really nice – how long have you been at it?
MARIGOLD	If you really want to know I got up at dawn.
POPPY	It certainly looks very impressive.
MARIGOLD	It ought to, the amount of work I've put into it.
POPPY	You look tired.
MARIGOLD	Thanks – and I've not finished yet.
POPPY	I don't know how you stay so keen.
MARIGOLD	I don't – I do it because that's what everyone expects, and I'll tell you something, I'm sick to the back teeth with it. I wouldn't mind but nobody seems to care that I've been slaving away all day.
POPPY	If you feel like that, why do you bother?
MARIGOLD	I sometimes ask myself that question.

(ALLYSSUM **is sitting cross-legged on the ground. She is staring intently at the Tree.** TANSY **and** PRIMROSE **are looking at her, they nudge each other, walk over and sit down beside her.**)

TANSY   What on earth are you doing?

ALLYSSUM   Sshh! I'm waiting for a vision.

PRIMROSE   What! *(Primrose and Tansy laugh.)*

ALLYSSUM   They do say that if you sit here on Treeday and stare at the Tree you'll get a vision of who you are going to marry.

PRIMROSE   Really?

ALLYSSUM   Yes, really.

PRIMROSE   Perhaps we should join you. Maybe we'll get a vision too. I've always wanted a vision. *(She looks at Tansy.)* Have you ever had a vision?

TANSY   Can't say I have, no.

(**They start to make fun of** ALLYSSUM. PRIMROSE **pretends to see something.**)

PRIMROSE   Look! Look! There!

ALLYSSUM   Where? *(She tries hard to see.)*

PRIMROSE   There. Can't you see? It's a face.

TANSY   Oh yes!

ALLYSSUM   Where? I can't see anything.

PRIMROSE   Oh dear, it's gone. It must have been for you. It couldn't have been for me – he had acne. *(Primrose and Tansy laugh.)*

TANSY   *(To Allyssum)* Hey, listen, do you fancy coming to a party?

PRIMROSE   That is if you're not too busy looking for visions.

ALLYSSUM   Yeh, OK – when?

TANSY   Tonight, after dark. *(She pauses.)* Here.

ALLYSSUM   What!

TANSY   Why not – it's a good place.

ALLYSSUM   Who else is going?

TANSY   Oh...loads of people.

PRIMROSE   I'll tell you what, we'll get Sorrel to go – I hear he's pretty good with visions.

ALLYSSUM   Oh alright.

(PRIMROSE **and** TANSY **leave** ALLYSSUM **staring up at the Tree. They walk over to where** SORREL **is working. The attention shifts to** ALDER **who is also decorating the glade.**)

ALDER   My father did this job and his father before him. This is our job and it's been in my family for as long as anyone can remember. Every year it's the same – every year the same.

(PRIMROSE **and** TANSY **walk up to** SORREL.)

TANSY   We've had this great idea – a party. That'll liven things up a bit.

SORREL   Terrific, count me in.

PRIMROSE   We're gonna show them how to celebrate.

SORREL   Lots of drink?

TANSY   Of course.

SORREL   Your place?

TANSY   No – here round the Tree.

SORREL   Are you out of your minds? You can't have a party here.

PRIMROSE   Why not?

SORREL   You know perfectly well why not.

TANSY   It would be a laugh.

SORREL   It would, wouldn't it – and we wouldn't actually be doing anything wrong, would we? *(Pause)* Are there going to be lots of girls?

PRIMROSE   Of course. You any good at visions?

SORREL   What?

PRIMROSE   I think Allyssum's interested in having a mystical experience with you.

(PRIMROSE, TANSY and SORREL go off to find other people to go to the party.)

JUNIPER   You any good at visions?

HYACINTH   What kind of visions?

JUNIPER   Visions of the future.

ALTHEA   I've got a crystal ball.

AMARYLLIS   Does it work?

ALTHEA   Not very well.

JUNIPER   Perhaps we should go to the party.

(POPPY walks up to COLUMBINE who is up a stepladder, decorating the glade.)

POPPY   Hi. *(She is looking a bit bored.)*

COLUMBINE   Hi. Happy Treeday. *(She points to a piece of the decoration she has just put up.)* What do you think of that?

POPPY   Fine.

COLUMBINE   You're sure it wouldn't be better up here? *(She holds the decoration a little higher.)*

POPPY   No, it's OK where it was. *(Pause)* I don't know how you manage to keep interested. I don't seem to have much enthusiasm these days. *(Pause)* And then there's all the work that has to be done.

COLUMBINE   You don't seem to be doing much.

POPPY   I can't be bothered.

COLUMBINE   Hold this for me would you. *(She gives Poppy a piece of decoration.)*

POPPY   Do you really believe in all this?

COLUMBINE   I suppose I do.

POPPY   Yeh – I suppose I do... really.

(COLUMBINE **continues to decorate the glade while** POPPY **watches. The attention shifts to** MOSS **and** BRYONY **who are surveying the scene.**)

MOSS   People don't seem to have enough respect these days.

BRYONY   That's because they take it all for granted.

MOSS   Well they shouldn't.

BRYONY   You can't blame people for being what they are.

MOSS   It's as if it isn't a religious duty anymore. They're not supposed to enjoy themselves, that's not the idea at all. I'll tell you something, if I were in charge I'd make them show respect.

(SORREL, PRIMROSE **and** TANSY **look over to** MOSS **and** BRYONY.**)**

TANSY   What about them?

PRIMROSE   Worth a try. *(They walk over.)*

TANSY   Hi. Fancy going to a party?

MOSS   I don't think so. I know what it will be like. You'll get drunk and get up to all manner of sinful things.

SORREL   Yes, with a bit of luck.

MOSS   Where is this party going to be held anyway?

TANSY   Oh... close by.

BRYONY   Where exactly?

TANSY   Well if you really want to know – it's going to be here, under the Tree, tonight.

MOSS   How dare you! This is absolutely and completely wrong! The whole idea is shameful!

PRIMROSE   Does that mean you're definitely not coming?

BRYONY   It's wrong and you know it is.

TANSY   We thought it might liven things up a bit.

BRYONY   It is possible to have a good time without overstepping the mark. Have your party, but not here – remember, this is a holy place.

(BRYONY **and** MOSS **walk off angrily.** ALDER **is still working.**)

ALDER   It's not a chore exactly but sometimes I wish I had a different job – a change is as good as a rest. But no – always this, every year the same.

(TANSY, SORREL **and** PRIMROSE **look over to where** BRACT **is working.**)

TANSY   What about asking Bract?

SORREL   You can't ask him – he'll do his nut.

PRIMROSE   Can't we – if we can get him to go, we can get anyone. Come on. *(They approach Bract.)* Hi Bract, Happy Treeday. *(Pause)* Listen, we've been talking and we've agreed that what we need is something to stimulate an interest in Treeday.

BRACT   They shouldn't need their interest stimulating, it should be enough that today is Treeday.

PRIMROSE   You're so right Bract but not everyone has your zeal, some of them have fallen by the wayside, so to speak.

TANSY   So we've planned a little celebration.

SORREL   A sort of a party.

PRIMROSE	*(Whispers to Sorrel)* Shut up!
BRACT	You know what I think about parties.
SORREL	Yes but this one would be rather special – we'd have it here round the Tree.
BRACT	I hope you're not serious.
SORREL	Yeh – why not?
BRACT	It would be blasphemous – forget the whole idea immediately.
SORREL	It would be just a little party.
BRACT	Drop the idea before it goes any further.
TANSY	You're only young once.
BRACT	Drop it!
TANSY	Alright.
PRIMROSE	Come on.

(PRIMROSE, TANSY **and** SORREL **exit.** BRACT **storms off. At this point in the play everyone has left the stage except for** ASPEN **and the** CHORUS. HOLLY **and** ASH **enter talking.)**

HOLLY	I've been thinking.
ASH	Careful.
HOLLY	You're asking for it, did you know that?
ASH	Chance would be a fine thing.
HOLLY	Right! *(She attacks him in a play fight.)*
ASH	Get off.
HOLLY	I'll teach you! *(She grabs his ear and twists it.)*
ASH	Alright, I give in. *(She lets go.)* What have you been thinking about – me I hope.
HOLLY	Don't be so conceited – I don't think about you all the time.

ASH   Only most of it, I hope. *(Pause)* Go on then, what is it?

HOLLY   You know all that about us living in the forest on our own – just us. Do you think it's true?

ASH   I don't know.

HOLLY   You must have some thoughts on the subject.

ASH   No.

HOLLY   We were born here. We live here. We'll die here. Sometimes it just doesn't seem enough.

ASH   I can't think about things like that. You know me – I even find getting up a problem.

HOLLY   But don't you even wonder?

ASH   It's no good asking me. You ought to try Aspen. *(Calls over to Aspen)* Aspen!

ASPEN   What?

ASH   Holly's got something to ask you.

HOLLY   No I haven't. *(She looks a bit worried about asking Aspen.)*

ASH   Yes you have – come on.

ASPEN   Well?

HOLLY   I know what it says in the stories but is it all true? Is there really only us or are there more people out there?

ASPEN   It is not possible to provide absolute answers but this much I will say – I find it difficult to believe that the Creator made all of this just for us. Strange that you should ask this question now because for some time I've had the feeling that we are not alone.

HOLLY   I feel it too. It's as if they're getting closer all the time.

ASH   Are you serious?

HOLLY   Oh yes.

ASPEN   We mustn't be surprised when we do eventually meet

them. It is important that we view the meeting with calmness and composure.

(HOLLY **and** ASH **exit.**)

JUNIPER Shall we tell the others?

HYACINTH Give them the news?

ASPEN Yes I think you should.

ALTHEA Getting closer, she said.

AMARYLLIS The feeling gets stronger.

JUNIPER A warning bell at the door.

HYACINTH What will they look like?

ALTHEA No one knows.

AMARYLLIS Re-adjust your mind: that's the custom.

JUNIPER Stay calm.

HYACINTH Composed.

ALTHEA Tranquil.

AMARYLLIS They'll mean us no harm.

JUNIPER We'd better go and tell the others.

AMARYLLIS Give them the news.

(**The** CHORUS **exit.**)

SCENE 2

ASPEN So the people contemplated an event outside their experience and then got on with the celebrations.

(**We hear the sound of music – the beating of a drum would be sufficient. The** PEOPLE **process in and take up a position.**)

ASPEN O great Tree, you stand firm against the wind and the rain! You hold the heavens, you fix the sky. Rising from the Earth you stand alone to give us life. We need the Tree.

THE PEOPLE   *(They shout the refrain.)* We need the Tree!

ASPEN   Listen – the Tree speaks, its soft words unfold to bring us life. Root of the world – accept now, on this our day of celebration, the gift of our gratitude. *(Pause)* Through time immemorial.

THE PEOPLE   The Tree!

ASPEN   Wondrous! Ethereal!

THE PEOPLE   The Tree!

ASPEN   Unceasing! Perpetual!

THE PEOPLE   The Tree!

ASPEN   We need the Tree!

THE PEOPLE   We need the Tree! We need the Tree! We need the Tree!

(As the shout dies away we hear the sound of an engine getting closer. Suddenly a dumper truck arrives with a SURVEY CREW seated on it. The PEOPLE turn to watch. When the engine is turned off there is a silence as the Crew and the People stare at each other.)

(If a dumper truck isn't available the Crew could simply walk on carrying the necessary survey equipment and some of the future references to the dumper truck can be cut, although many of them will still work without a visible truck.)

FORD   Wow! Locals!

MORRIS   Oh Lord, I hope they're not hostile.

BENTLEY   Do they look hostile?

MORRIS   Looks can be very deceptive.

RILEY   Quiet, aren't they?

AUSTIN   Well as it says in the manual, 'If in doubt, attempt communication'. Leave this to me. *(He walks over to the People.)* Me – civil engineer. *(He points at himself.)* We come in peace.

(There is no response from the PEOPLE. **They stare in silence at the** CREW.**)**

MORRIS   Isn't it important to smile? Did you know that the smile is one of the few cross-cultural indicators of friendship? Apparently smiling is common to all societies.

RILEY   Really?

MORRIS   Yeh – I read it in the *Readers' Digest.*

AUSTIN   I'll give it a try. *(He grins like an idiot.)* Me – road builder.

FORD   You don't seem to be getting through, boss.

AUSTIN   OK then, you try.

(FORD walks over to TANSY.**)**

FORD   Hi there honey. Me one very laid back super cool civil engineer – you one very gorgeous girl. Me come in peace and love – especially love. What say you to a little stroll in the woods? *(Tansy gives him a hard stare but says nothing.)*

AUSTIN   Forget it. Pass me the radio. *(Bentley hands him a walkie-talkie.)* Survey Team to base. Survey Team to base. Over. *(There is a pause while he listens.)* We're at map reference 2395–4266. You got that? Over. *(Pause)* We've got a slight problem; we've run into some locals and we don't know how to deal with them. Can you send us someone who knows what they're doing? Over. *(Pause)* As soon as possible. Thanks.

BENTLEY   Now what?

AUSTIN   We sit and wait.

MORRIS   Come on, guys – let's all give them a smile. Say 'curly-wurly'? *(He grins and looks at the Crew. They give him a look of disdain. Pause.)*

CLEOME   We've been expecting you.

MORRIS   See – smiling does work.

CLEOME   You or someone like you.

(The Crew look at each other in astonishment.)

AUSTIN   But you speak our language.

CLEOME   Perhaps it's you who speak ours.

AUSTIN   Why didn't you speak straightaway?

CLEOME   We wanted to make sure you weren't hostile.

MORRIS   Do we look hostile?

CLEOME   Looks can be very deceptive.

AUSTIN   Well I suppose we'd better introduce ourselves. We work for International Transportation Services and we're here on behalf of your government. Are you the chief?

CLEOME   Chief?

AUSTIN   You know – the leader.

CLEOME   I am this year's elected speaker if that's what you mean.

BENTLEY   I bet you don't see many strangers, do you?

CLEOME   None.

AUSTIN   I see – well you're going to have to realise that you are now part of a very big world with lots of people in it.

BRACT   You mean there are more of you out there?

FORD   Just a few.

AUSTIN   It looks like we are your first point of contact with civilisation. In years to come you'll look back on this moment as the major event in your history. And what is more we are here to give you something – a road! You see, we are building a road through this forest.

BENTLEY We've already built seven hundred kilometres – there's only another six hundred to go. It's a fantastic feat of engineering. A marvel of the age.

AUSTIN It travels in a dead straight line from East to West. There are no curves, no bends – every centimetre is dead on track. A thin black line slicing through the green pageant of the primeval forest.

BENTLEY It's a three-lane motorway – with hard shoulders.

MORRIS And service stations – don't forget the service stations.

BENTLEY You will be amazed, absolutely amazed. And it's all heading your way.

CLEOME And you five will do all that?

BENTLEY Oh no – there are lots more of us. We are just the advance guard.

AUSTIN This place could become very important.

MORRIS And if you're very lucky they might even build you a service station right here.

AUSTIN Just think of the jobs that will bring. You'd better realise that from now on things are going to be different around here.

BRACT Cleome – a word. *(He has been standing well away from the Crew and obviously regards them with suspicion.)*

CLEOME Excuse me a moment.

(She walks over to BRACT. The PEOPLE **turn to watch and to listen.)**

BENTLEY What's going on?

AUSTIN Search me.

BENTLEY Trouble?

AUSTIN I don't know.

(The PEOPLE **have a discussion.)**

BRACT We need to talk about the strangers.

CLEOME I know, but in the meantime what do we do with them?

ASPEN Whatever we do we must not forget our manners. We need to reassure them and show them that we mean them no harm.

CLEOME You're right.

(CLEOME turns towards the CREW**.)**

Gentlemen, you are welcome. If you would like to come with us we will take you to our village where you can rest after your journey and take some food with us.

AUSTIN *(The Crew look at each other.)* Yeh – OK, thanks very much.

POPPY If you'd like to come this way.

(The CREW **and the** PEOPLE **exit, leaving** BRACT **and** CLEOME**.)**

BRACT At least while they're in the village we can keep an eye on them.

CLEOME Why are you so suspicious? They seem friendly enough.

BRACT Just prudence, that's all.

(BRACT and CLEOME **exit.)**

JUNIPER It was just as you said. How do you do it?

ASPEN Well I don't read tea leaves.

HYACINTH And now?

ALTHEA What now?

AMARYLLIS What does it all mean?

JUNIPER	A million questions fired like shooting stars, bounding and rebounding.
HYACINTH	Tell us the future, Aspen.
ASPEN	There are bound to be changes.
ALTHEA	Absolutely.
ASPEN	Alterations to our lives.
AMARYLLIS	That's plain to see.
JUNIPER	A multitude of thoughts crowding, jostling, pushing for position.
HYACINTH	What can we learn from them?
ALTHEA	What can they learn from us?
AMARYLLIS	What do we want from them?
JUNIPER	What do they want from us?
HYACINTH	A crack in the fabric – a chink of light.
ALTHEA	More like a flash of lightning.
AMARYLLIS	Re-adjust your mind, that's the custom.
JUNIPER	Did you see the machine, the noise it made, the way it moved?
HYACINTH	Their clothes, the way they look, the way they speak.
ALTHEA	They speak like us.
HYACINTH	We speak like them.
ALTHEA	There are more of them out there.
AMARYLLIS	So they say.
JUNIPER	They exude strangeness.
HYACINTH	A peculiarity.
ALTHEA	The word is 'odd'.
AMARYLLIS	We'd better keep an eye on them.

SCENE 3

(ALDER **enters with a wheelbarrow – he starts to clear away.**)

ALDER   Tradition is all very well but it does have its own momentum – or lack of momentum – depending on which way you look at it. It's a kind of active inertia, a constant reminder that we are standing still. My family have tidied up this spot for as long as anyone can remember. My father did it and his father before him. Every year the same. Every year the same.

(ALDER **exits with decorations in his wheelbarrow.**)

SCENE 4

(BRYONY **and** COLUMBINE **enter. They have come to take down the decorations.** FORD, MORRIS **and** RILEY **follow them on.**)

FORD   Hi there girls. *(The girls ignore him. He walks over to Bryony.)* Hey baby, how would you like to come for a little spin in my dumper truck? Maybe we could park up somewhere and slip into the back seat.

MORRIS   It doesn't have a back seat, remember.

FORD   That is a minor detail – we'll use the bucket up-front instead. The concrete may be a little rough but we'll make out. What d'ya say, baby? I'll show you a real good time.

BRYONY   Oh yes?

FORD   Oh yes!

BRYONY   I don't quite understand. What do you mean – 'a real good time'?

FORD   Come off it, I know what you primitives are like – I've seen it in the *National Geographic*.

BRYONY   I'm still not sure what you're talking about – you see I'm only a poor primitive. What exactly do you mean?

FORD   You know...love...romance...amour...nooky!

BRYONY   Oh I see. But you haven't told me your name.

FORD   The name, baby, is Ford. *(He takes her hand and looks deep into her eyes.)*

BRYONY   Well Ford, if you don't take your hands off me I'm going to knee you where it hurts. *(She snatches her hand away.)*

FORD   Playing hard to get, huh?

BRYONY   In your case I'm playing impossible to get.

MORRIS   Why don't you show her your theodolyte?

FORD   Can I help it if she has no taste? *(He turns to Columbine.)* What about you honey? You look like the kind of girl who could handle some fun.

RILEY   Leave it out Ford, enough's enough, eh?

COLUMBINE   It's comforting to know that these men behave just the same as the ones we know and love. In a rapidly changing world, that's something.

(AUSTIN and BENTLEY enter.)

AUSTIN   Where the hell did you get to, then?

FORD   Oh, we've just been engaging the locals in a little polite chit-chat.

JUNIPER   What's out there? We want to know. *(The Crew turn to look at the Chorus.)*

BENTLEY   We ought to tell them.

AUSTIN   You're right, we should.

BRYONY   Isn't this something we should all hear?

ASPEN   Yes. Go and fetch everyone.

BRYONY   *(To Columbine)* Come on.

(COLUMBINE **and** BRYONY **exit.)**

AUSTIN   *(To the Chorus)* Can I ask you something?

HYACINTH   Of course.

AUSTIN   I want to know why you weren't surprised when we arrived.

HYACINTH   Aspen told us you would come.

AUSTIN   What's she, some kind of witchdoctor?

HYACINTH   Not really.

RILEY   And you took it all so calmly – we burst in and you don't even bat an eyelid.

JUNIPER   That's our way in all things. We do our best to stay calm.

AMARYLLIS   But it's not always easy.

RILEY   How do you live? You don't seem to farm or anything.

ALTHEA   The forest gives us everything and in return we watch over the Tree.

MORRIS   I bet you talk to the trees.

ALTHEA   When necessary.

RILEY   *(Whispers to Morris)* Shut up!

JUNIPER   We are the Guardians of the Tree.

AUSTIN   Which tree?

JUNIPER   That Tree! *(She points at the Tree.)* The Tree that supports the sky. Without the Tree the sky would fall and it would be the end of everything.

MORRIS   Chicken licken rides again.

RILEY   Morris!

AUSTIN You really believe that?

JUNIPER Oh yes.

RILEY What do you do here? How do you pass the time?

AMARYLLIS We collect food, we look after the village, we make things, we marry, we have children.

HYACINTH We grow old.

FORD Yeh, but what do you do for fun?

HYACINTH We paint.

ALTHEA Tell stories.

AMARYLLIS We make music.

FORD Do you dance?

AMARYLLIS Sometimes.

FORD I know, you have exotic ceremonies in which you cover your bodies with oil to make them glisten and then you dance in the firelight to the throbbing beat of the tom-toms.

AMARYLLIS All the time.

FORD Dull old life you lead.

(HOLLY **enters followed by** BRYONY **and the rest of the** PEOPLE.)

HOLLY What is it like out there?

JUNIPER You did say you'd tell us.

BENTLEY Out there is civilisation. Out there is...television! And radio...and video.

AUSTIN Motorcars and motorbikes.

BENTLEY Microwaves and automatic washing machines.

FORD Stephen Spielberg.

MORRIS Coca-Cola.

BENTLEY BBC, ITV and...PTFE!

MORRIS PTFE?

BENTLEY Yeh – polytetrafluorethylene. You know, the black stuff they put on frying pans to stop your eggs sticking.

MORRIS Gee thanks, I'm sure that piece of priceless information will come in very useful.

BENTLEY And then of course there's...Corn Flakes, low-fat yoghurt, cigarettes, McDonald's, hairspray, aeroplanes...the list is endless.

AUSTIN And all that civilisation is just for starters – we haven't even begun to tell you what's out there.

BENTLEY And what's more it's going to come rolling down the road, just for you! What do you think about that then?

HYACINTH It'll mean a few changes.

BENTLEY The improvement in your lifestyle will be phenomenal.

HOLLY This road, will we be able to travel on it?

BENTLEY Oh yes.

HOLLY How soon will it get here?

AUSTIN This section is due for completion within the next three months.

ASPEN What's on your mind?

HOLLY Nothing.

AUSTIN Anything else you want to know?

JUNIPER I think you've told us enough.

HYACINTH For the moment.

AUSTIN Don't hesitate to ask if you've got any more questions.

ALTHEA Oh we won't.

AUSTIN Good. *(Pause)* Well if you'll excuse us we've got some surveying to do.

(AUSTIN **motions to the** CREW **and they exit.)**

SCENE 5

JUNIPER	So what do we think about all that?
HYACINTH	It's all going to be ours.
ALTHEA	So they tell us.
AMARYLLIS	What we need is a meeting.
JUNIPER	How right you are. *(She calls)* Cleome!
CLEOME	What?
JUNIPER	We need a meeting. What do you say?
CLEOME	I say, let all who wish it speak their minds.
PRIMROSE	This could be the best thing that ever happened. I say we take what's on offer.
BRYONY	We should keep our distance.
POPPY	We must beware the discontent. They must not unsettle us.
SORREL	We can have civilisation. They said so.
MARIGOLD	I'm happy with the way things are.
ALLYSSUM	What visions will they bring me?
ALDER	I have a feeling they're going to make a mess. Who's going to clear up? That's what I want to know.
HOLLY	I want to see the world that's out there.
ASH	I don't know what I think.
TANSY	It's exciting out there and it's pretty boring here.
BRACT	I don't trust them – at all!
COLUMBINE	I think they might provide me with some interesting opportunities.

MOSS   Why are they so superior, that's what I want to know?

JUNIPER   Change is dangerous. Maybe we should live a little dangerously.

HYACINTH   I think they're wonderful.

ALTHEA   It could be very amusing.

AMARYLLIS   I wonder if they know any good jokes? I bet they do.

CLEOME   The situation may prove to our ultimate advantage. *(She looks at Aspen.)* What do you say, Aspen?

ASPEN   I say that for each new event there are four boxes from which to pick an answer. The first box is marked...

JUNIPER   Absolute inevitability.

ASPEN   Then there is the box marked...

HYACINTH   Ignore the event.

ASPEN   And the box marked...

ALTHEA   Compromise and adjust.

ASPEN   And finally the box marked...

AMARYLLIS   Those things worth dying for.

ASPEN   The last to be used sparingly. The trick is to pick from the right box at the right time.

(The PEOPLE look at each other for a moment. Then they exit talking about what they are going to do. COLUMBINE is left on stage – she is looking at the dumper truck. RILEY enters; he has come to pick up something from the truck. He sees COLUMBINE and stops. He approaches her tentatively.)

RILEY   My name's Riley. What's yours?

COLUMBINE   Columbine.

RILEY   That's a nice name.

COLUMBINE Is it? We're all named after the plants of the forest. Some of us have quite awful names.

RILEY I'm sorry about Ford – the way he behaved.

COLUMBINE He's alright – he seems harmless enough. That machine, what does it do? *(She indicates the dumper truck.)*

RILEY It's called a dumper truck. We use it for ferrying small loads around the site. Sometimes we ride about on it – it's very useful for short journeys.

COLUMBINE When I listened to you all talking about your world I could feel my world shrinking as you spoke. If I thought about it I could be frightened. We could be overwhelmed.

RILEY You could ignore us – pretend we don't exist and go deeper into the forest.

COLUMBINE We couldn't leave here. Who'd look after the Tree – you? *(Pause)* Today's Treeday. Did you know that?

RILEY No.

COLUMBINE It's the day when we celebrate the sowing of the seed from which the Tree grew. Do you have Treeday?

RILEY We have something like it but it doesn't have much significance these days.

COLUMBINE *(Pause)* Would you like to see my house?

RILEY Please.

COLUMBINE It's at its best today. We clean everything from top to bottom ready to begin the new year. I wonder what this year will bring.

RILEY It'll bring the road, that's for sure.

COLUMBINE What's really going to happen to us?

RILEY You'll be alright.

(RILEY and COLUMBINE **walk off.)**

SCENE 6

(ALDER **enters with his wheelbarrow.**)

ALDER   Everyone's falling down on the job. What is the world coming to? Somebody's going to have to clear up. *(He starts to take the decorations off the Tree.)* I shouldn't be tidying the Tree. It's not really my job. It comes to a pretty pass when you've got to do other people's work as well as your own. *(Pause)* Still it does make a change.

(POPPY **enters.**)

POPPY   What are you doing?

ALDER   What does it look like?

POPPY   I didn't know that was your job.

ALDER   It's not.

POPPY   What do you think about all the things the strangers said?

ALDER   Look at it this way, if only half of what they told us is true it's going to mean a lot of changes.

POPPY   It does open up a lot of possibilities, doesn't it?

ALDER   You can say that again.

(**Enter** PRIMROSE, COLUMBINE **and** TANSY.)

PRIMROSE   Hey, guess what? One of them has just promised me a ride on his machine.

POPPY   Which one?

PRIMROSE   Ford.

POPPY   I've heard about him. You want to be careful.

PRIMROSE   Why should I? You're only young once.

ALDER   You're asking for trouble, do you know that? You've no idea what he might be up to.

COLUMBINE   True – but it might be fun finding out.

ALDER   You wouldn't go out with me when I asked you.

POPPY   Ah, but you haven't got a big machine.

ALDER   How do you know?

TANSY   When the road comes and it brings all those things they promised what are you going to have? I'm going to have a car. You can get them in any colour, they told me. I think I'd like a green one to match the leaves.

POPPY   Where would you go in this car?

TANSY   I'd go out there – down the road. I'd see for myself what it's like.

ALDER   Do you think we can have anything we want?

TANSY   I suppose so.

ALDER   In that case, if you're going to have a car, I'm going to have a motorbike. It's like a car only faster, that's what they said.

TANSY   What about you?

POPPY   I don't know.

TANSY   Come on, play the game.

POPPY   Right – if you're going to have a car, and you're going to have a motorbike, I'm going to have a...microwave.

ALDER   What's a microwave?

POPPY   I don't know, but it sounds good and everybody's getting one, they told me.

TANSY   *(To Primrose)* What are you going to have?

POPPY   She means apart from Ford, that is.

PRIMROSE   You be quiet – you're only jealous.

ALDER   Come on then, what's it to be?

PRIMROSE   I'll have a car as well.

TANSY   You can't because I've already picked one and the rules of the game say you can't pick anything that someone has already picked.

PRIMROSE   What rules?

TANSY   My game – my rules.

ASPEN   What are the rules of the game?

JUNIPER   No one knows.

ALTHEA   Your game.

AMARYLLIS   Your rules.

HYACINTH   Well?

TANSY   Oh, alright then, you can have anything you want.

ASPEN   You heard, you can have anything you want.

JUNIPER   All we have to do is to take advantage of what's on offer.

HYACINTH   Snap up the bargains.

ALTHEA   Grab them while they're hot.

ASPEN   And the price?

AMARYLLIS   What price?

ASPEN   The price to pay – there's always a price to pay. Something for nothing, that's not their way.

(ALDER, POPPY, TANSY **and** COLUMBINE **exit.**)

SCENE 7

(SORREL, ALLYSSUM, HOLLY **and** ASH **enter.**)

SORREL   We've made up our minds: we're going to leave.

ALLYSSUM   People keep telling us to grow up and settle down but

I don't want that. I don't know what I want but it isn't that.

HOLLY   When are you going?

SORREL   As soon as we can. They said we can have a lift out when the rest of the transport arrives.

ALLYSSUM We're going to find out for ourselves what's out there. It's like we've been shut up in a dark room all this time while outside the sun has been shining. Now we're going to open the door and let the light come flooding in. Why don't you come with us? We could all go.

ASH   I don't know.

HOLLY   Please Ash, we could. I don't want to stay cooped up here knowing exactly what the future will bring – it's all so predictable. *(Pause)* Please!

ASH   I suppose we could always come back if it doesn't work out.

HOLLY   So we can go?

ASH   If that's what you want.

HOLLY   You know it is.

ASH   What will we do out there?

HOLLY   I don't know – does it matter? If we don't take a few risks now, we never will.

ASH   But what if it all goes wrong?

SORREL   So what if we fail, at least we'll have had a go.

ALLYSSUM If we're not prepared to gamble we won't ever win anything.

HOLLY   She's right, can't you see that?

ASH   OK, I said I'm going.

HOLLY   You don't sound very enthusiastic.

ASH   I'll work on it.

(They exit.)

SCENE 8

(Enter ALLARD **and** SCOTT.**)**

ALLARD   Look, there's the truck but where are the crew? Perhaps they've been eaten. I can just imagine it – fricassee of survey crew with a few French fries and asparagus tips.

SCOTT   Look – there are no cannibals in this forest.

ALLARD   So you tell me.

SCOTT   They've probably wandered off.

ALLARD   They've no business wandering off and leaving company property unattended, not with hostiles about.

SCOTT   I do wish you'd stop referring to the indigenous population as hostiles. We don't know for certain that they are and, until we find out to the contrary, the best course of action is to assume they're peaceful.

ALLARD   Well I'm not so sure. Remember we're dealing with primitives. We have to be very careful here – a few precautions wouldn't come amiss. Have a look at this. *(She reaches into her handbag and produces a revolver.)* It's called a 'Saturday night special' – more of a fashion accessory really, but very effective. I bought it the last time I was in New York – they're all the rage. In my experience, and I've been responsible for building roads on every continent of this planet, the only way to be certain is with something like this.

SCOTT   I don't agree and remember I'm paid to advise on these matters.

ALLARD   And you remember that I'm paid to make decisions

and I can ignore your advice if I want to. *(She puts the revolver away.)*

SCOTT   Look, have you seen this tree? *(She indicates the Tree.)*

ALLARD   Who do you think left all that rubbish round it? *(She means the decorations.)*

SCOTT   The inhabitants most likely. It's probably the remains of some kind of ceremony. Animism is very common amongst forest-dwelling peoples.

ALLARD   Animism?

SCOTT   Yes – the belief that all living things have a soul and are sacred.

ALLARD   Even trees?

SCOTT   Especially trees, I would think.

ALLARD   What a silly idea.

SCOTT   I wish you wouldn't be so dismissive – it's probably quite natural if you live in a forest.

ALLARD   Like I said – primitives.

SCOTT   They may have a highly developed civilisation for all you know.

ALLARD   When they can build roads then they're civilised but until that time comes, in my book, they're primitive. *(Pause)* Come on, let's go find the survey crew.

(ALLARD and SCOTT **exit.)**

SCENE 9

(Enter RILEY **and** COLUMBINE.**)**

RILEY   It's wonderful.

COLUMBINE   You think so?

RILEY   Oh yes – absolutely. It's all so natural. You live here in peace and harmony with the forest.

COLUMBINE   Really?

RILEY   You lack for nothing – the forest provides you with everything. It's beautiful.

COLUMBINE   And you liked my house?

RILEY   It was perfect in its simplicity.

COLUMBINE   Is there anything else you'd like to see? *(She looks at Riley and smiles.)*

RILEY   I don't think so. *(He looks blank; he totally misses the point of what she is saying.)*

COLUMBINE   Well...er...I could show you the forest. *(She smiles and looks at Riley again)*...but then I expect you've seen a forest before.

RILEY   *(Very enthusiastic; he's probably an amateur naturalist.)* Ah yes, but not with one of you as a guide. I bet you know all the footpaths and the places where the wild flowers grow and the animals live. The forest is your domain isn't it? Yes, it would be very interesting to see the forest, thank you.

COLUMBINE   OK then, I'll show you the forest. *(She looks disappointed.)*

(RILEY and COLUMBINE start to leave when ALLARD and SCOTT enter from the other side of the clearing.)

ALLARD   Hey Riley! It is Riley, isn't it?

RILEY   Oh dear, that's Allard. She's from head office. I think you'll have to show me round later. The other one must be the company anthropologist. I'd forgotten that we'd radioed for help.

SCOTT   *(To Allard)* Leave this to me.

(SCOTT walks forward to meet COLUMBINE. Scott shows an upright raised palm to indicate peace. She takes some beads from her bag.)

We come in peace! See we bring gifts. *(She offers the beads to Columbine.)*

COLUMBINE Thank you very much. My name's Columbine. You must be the company anthropologist. *(She takes the beads and puts them on. Scott is dumbstruck.)*

RILEY It's alright, we speak the same language.

SCOTT How absolutely amazing. I always knew it was statistically possible for two separate cultures to evolve the same language but I never thought I'd see it for myself.

ALLARD Where are the others?

RILEY At the village – we've been telling them about the road.

SCOTT That's really my job you know. *(She looks a little hurt.)*

RILEY Sorry, but you weren't here. It seemed the best thing to do.

ALLARD What are you doing here on your own, with her – or needn't I ask?

RILEY She was showing me round – it was very interesting.

ALLARD I bet it was.

SCOTT Do you think she'd show me round? I'd like to take some photos, maybe even conduct a few interviews. It would be useful at this stage to make a record for posterity.

RILEY You'd better ask her yourself.

(Scott looks at Columbine.)

COLUMBINE I will if you want.

ALLARD Before we all go sightseeing I'd like to get down to business. I want to meet the rest of your village. Can you fix it?

COLUMBINE   I'll go and tell them you're here.

RILEY   You'd better bring my friends as well.

(COLUMBINE **exits.**)

ALLARD   Look Riley, what exactly is the situation here? Are they hostile?

RILEY   No – the opposite if anything.

ALLARD   That's nice to know. I couldn't cope with any more delays. The geological sub-stratum hasn't been all it should. We've had serious subsidence problems ninety kilometres back.

RILEY   We had heard.

ALLARD   You know you might have solved a little problem for me. I've been looking for a site for the next construction camp and you seem to have stumbled on the ideal position. How do you think they'll take to a couple of hundred construction workers moving in here?

RILEY   They're very hospitable but that might be stretching things a bit.

SCOTT   You must realise that if you do something like that the culture shock will be tremendous.

ALLARD   They're going to have to get used to it sooner or later – the sooner the better if you ask me. Besides if we put the camp here we can keep an eye on them.

(**The** PEOPLE **and the** CREW **enter.**)

JUNIPER   Another step along the way.

HYACINTH   A meeting between us and them.

ALTHEA   A meeting of minds?

AMARYLLIS   You think so?

ALTHEA   No!

AUSTIN   *(He sees Allard.)* Oh Lord, what's she doing here? I asked for help not hindrance.

SCOTT   Greetings. My name is Scott. This is Allard, a big chief from the company.

CLEOME   We are the People. I am called Cleome. We are pleased to see you. We have had a meeting and we have decided that the best policy is to accept the road and to face up to the challenge and the change it will bring. It is our way to compromise in all things.

JUNIPER   Re-adjust the mind – that's the way.

HYACINTH   A bit of the old – a bit of the new.

ALTHEA   A house of fresh ideas to dwell in.

BRACT   Not all of us are so sure, are we Cleome?

CLEOME   Nevertheless we are agreed – the will of the majority rules, that is the custom.

SCOTT   That is a very constructive attitude to take if I may say so. I am here to help you to adapt. If there is anything you do not understand, you must come to me and I will explain. I hope that in the future we can work together to ensure that you continue the progress of adaptation in the smooth way you have already begun it.

ALLARD   Oh and by the way – we're going to build our next construction site here.

SCOTT   That is, if you have no objection. *(She gives Allard a dirty look.)*

ALLARD   And another thing. I've just noticed that this tree here is right in the path of the road. *(She indicates the Tree.)* It's going to have to come down – that is, if you have no objection.

(The People look at each other in astonishment.)

JUNIPER   Did you hear? It trips so easily off the tongue.

HYACINTH   The Tree is in the way.

AMARYLLIS   It will have to come down.

ALTHEA   That is, if we have no objection.

JUNIPER   It trips so easily off the tongue.

CLEOME   Do I hear you right? You want to cut down the Tree?

ALLARD   That's correct.

BRACT   She's either a fool or she's making fun of us.

CLEOME   Do you know what the Tree does?

ALLARD   I know exactly what it does – it gets in the way and that means it's going to have to come down. As far as I'm concerned it isn't any different from the million or so other trees that we've uprooted to get to this point.

SCOTT   I get the impression that this tree is an important part of their value system – it's obviously some sort of holy tree. Couldn't we just put a little curve in the road, you know, just round the tree?

ALLARD   Unfortunately not. A detour would cost time and money. And besides I can just see my report to the General Manager: 'Look Mr Packard, I'm sorry that the road isn't the dead straight line you were promised but you see there was this holy tree that we just had to build round.' Perhaps you'd like to tell him?

SCOTT   But we really ought to do something – you never know, the situation could turn nasty. They're obviously very touchy about it. Trouble could mean delay and we don't want that, do we?

BRACT   Do you have to talk about us as if we don't exist?!

ALLARD   I was under the impression you didn't and according to my map you don't. This area is designated as being uninhabited. *(Bract walks away in disgust.)*

SCOTT   Listen I've had an idea. We could move the tree! We

put it somewhere out of the way. There is a small budget for that sort of thing.

ALLARD   Well done, problem solved. That's settled then, we'll move the tree and then we're all happy, you get to keep your tree and I get to keep the road on schedule.

CLEOME   You don't understand! The Tree cannot be moved!

ALLARD   Of course it can. We've got the technology.

CLEOME   *(She looks to Aspen.)* She is impossible. How do I make her understand?

ASPEN   That tree, unlike the many you have already destroyed, is not an ordinary tree.

ALLARD   It's a holy tree, I understand that. And believe me I'm not unsympathetic. But like I said, there is no problem. You can keep your tree, only it will have to be moved.

ASPEN   No! It will not be moved! It is the Tree that holds up the Sky. Take it away and the sky will fall and that will mean the end of all things – even of you and your road.

ALLARD   You expect me to believe that?

ASPEN   Some important things are difficult to believe, but without a belief in something greater than ourselves we are empty and hollow. We are dry people who can be blown away. The more difficult the belief the greater must be the faith, that is the nature of the exercise. I believe in the Creator and I believe in the Tree. Tell me, what do you believe in?

ALLARD   I believe in progress, that's what I believe in. Ever since human beings came down out of the trees we have been advancing. Now, for the first time, it is within our grasp to tame this planet and to use it for the benefit of all humankind. We could leave this forest alone, but why should we? It was put here to use – it must not be left to waste. The road is the way forward; that tree is the way back. You have a clear choice –

you can adapt or you can disappear. That has always been the choice and you'd better face up to it. So what's it to be? Does the tree simply come down or do we move it for you? All other options are out. And now I'm going to take a little look around. I've got a few preparations to make.

(ALLARD **walks out.** SCOTT **looks a little embarrassed, she looks uncertainly round her and then follows Allard. The** CREW **look at each other and at the** PEOPLE**, some of whom are looking bewildered and some are looking angry.)**

AUSTIN   I think we'd better make ourselves scarce.

(The CREW **exit.)**

JUNIPER   Events gather apace.

HYACINTH   You can adjust to anything if you try hard enough.

ALTHEA   It's simply a question of refocussing the mind.

AMARYLLIS   But this... what now? *(She looks at Aspen.)*

JUNIPER   It was all just a game... but what now? *(She too looks at Aspen.)*

HYACINTH   What picture do you see Aspen? *(The People are all looking at Aspen.)*

ASPEN   I see the tall flames burning, the hard flood running, the trees falling like bodies. I see the grass die, crying, the dead skin shrivel, the birds flying like stones. I see the corpses of the morning with mouths that cannot scream.

(Everyone walks out slowly and silently.)

End of Act One

ACT TWO

SCENE 1

(**The** PEOPLE **enter.** ASPEN **and the** CHORUS **take up their positions.**)

ASPEN   It is often the case that we don't truly value those things that are really precious until someone wants to take them away.

AMARYLLIS   What's the price we have to pay? Something for nothing, that's not their way.

ALTHEA   It was all just a game, that's all – just a game.

JUNIPER   But now?

HYACINTH   What now?

BRACT   Well Cleome, how do we handle this one?

CLEOME   Don't look to me for an answer, I'm just the Speaker, remember.

BRACT   What do you suggest – that we ignore them and hope they'll go away?

CLEOME   I don't know.

POPPY   What frightens me is that they're so certain that they're right.

SORREL   What happens if they are and it's us that are wrong?

BRYONY   Of course we're not wrong.

TANSY   Are you sure? Maybe it's time to say out loud what many of us have been thinking for some time. Who still believes in the Tree? I don't. I never have, not since I was a child.

SORREL   Nor me.

PRIMROSE Lots of us feel the same.

TANSY   Open your eyes and look at it – can't you see it's
          nothing but a piece of wood? How can it hold up the
          sky? It's just a myth. The story isn't true.

BRYONY   Yes it is! I believe every word of it!

TANSY   Well lots of us don't.

PRIMROSE And some of us don't care.

BRYONY   How can you say that?

PRIMROSE Easy – I just open my mouth. It's like they said, the
          future is out there and I'm going to take full advantage
          of it.

BRYONY   If they chop the Tree down there'll be nothing to take
          advantage of!

CLEOME   I ask again, what are we going to do? In the past we
          have always solved problems by compromise – what is
          the compromise here?

BRACT   The problem with compromise is that you have to
          know when to stop. There is no compromise.

CLEOME   Then what do you suggest we do?

BRACT   I would have thought it was pretty obvious – we have
          to fight!

MOSS   He's right.

POPPY   We can't – it's against custom.

BRACT   If the Tree comes down, there'll be no custom.

POPPY   Then we'll have to try to stop them without using
          violence.

MOSS   And how do you propose to do that?

POPPY   I don't know.

BRACT   No, we have to fight – there is no other way.

POPPY   What will you fight with? You haven't got any weapons.

BRACT   I'll make one. I'll go into the forest and find a tall straight sapling and make myself a spear. The wood of the forest will defend the Tree – appropriate don't you think.

MOSS   We'll all make one.

CLEOME   No! We must keep talking to them. We must make them realise.

BRACT   You can talk all you want, but me, I'm going to do something. I'm not prepared to watch the world fall apart.

MOSS   I'm with you.

BRYONY   And me.

BRACT   *(He looks up at the Chorus.)* Whose side are you on?

JUNIPER   We haven't made up our minds yet.

HYACINTH   We're still thinking about it.

MOSS   While you're thinking about it we're going to fight for what we believe in.

(BRACT, MOSS **and** BRYONY **storm out. MARIGOLD looks confused, she hesitates and then makes a decision.)**

MARIGOLD   Wait for me.

(MARIGOLD **runs out.)**

ASH   Come on! *(He looks at Holly.)*

HOLLY   No, I'm staying.

ASH   Please.

HOLLY   No.

(ASH **looks unhappy. He looks at** HOLLY **for a moment, then he turns and walks out after the others.)**

TANSY   Good riddance I say.

POPPY   Don't.

TANSY   Why not? It's sickening the way you all cling to the past. You're not afraid of losing the Tree, you're afraid of the future. Me, I've seen enough of the Tree, I'm going – I think I'll start packing.

(TANSY **exits and** PRIMROSE **goes with her.**)

SORREL   Talk about gloom and doom. What happened to the party spirit, that's what I want to know. I think we should let things take their course. It'll be alright in the end. *(He looks at Allyssum.)* Come on, we'd better get packed as well.

(SORREL **and** ALLYSSUM **exit, followed by** HOLLY.)

ALDER   Where does that leave us?

POPPY   I don't know. I just know it's wrong to fight. Have you ever thought that if we do use violence maybe we deserve to lose the Tree.

CLEOME   *(To the Chorus)* What about you?

ALTHEA   We're still not sure.

CLEOME   You will let us know when you've made up your minds, won't you? *(She looks a little impatient.)*

(CLEOME, POPPY **and** ALDER **exit.** COLUMBINE **is now alone on the stage.** ASPEN **looks down at her.**)

ASPEN   And you, what do you say?

COLUMBINE   *(She smiles.)* Me – I've got my own plans.

(COLUMBINE **exits.**)

SCENE 2

JUNIPER   Has the end already begun?

HYACINTH   Listen to us argue.

AMARYLLIS	It was never like this before.
ALTHEA	Tell us the future, Aspen.
ASPEN	I told you, I don't read tea leaves.
JUNIPER	It's important for us to know.
HYACINTH	We want to gauge the odds.
AMARYLLIS	Hedge our bets.
ALTHEA	If we're going to risk everything, what do we stand to gain?

(SCOTT enters.)

SCOTT	When the tree has come down and you realise that everything is fine you will be able to start a new life. I must say it's very wise of you to think about the future.
JUNIPER	Do you read tea leaves?
SCOTT	What?
JUNIPER	The future, tell us about the future!
SCOTT	I am sure that the government will allow you to keep much of the land here. You will be able to clear the forest, plant crops and farm. Some of you will even be able to get jobs at the service station once you've had a little training. Which is where I come in. I thought we'd begin with a few pictures of the outside world. We call them photographs.
AMARYLLIS	They call them photographs.
SCOTT	They're part of the education programme that is designed to give you an understanding of the outside world. Soon I'll get literacy classes underway and then you'll all be able to learn to read and write.
ALTHEA	And we'll become like you?
SCOTT	In time, yes.

JUNIPER   With all the things you have?

SCOTT   It's all possible, the opportunities are there – it's simply a question of re-adjustment.

ALTHEA   We know all that – it's the custom here.

JUNIPER   Do I detect a little cynicism?

ALTHEA   Not at all.

(SCOTT **looks a little bemused as she exits.**)

SCENE 3

(PRIMROSE **enters. She's come to meet** FORD. **She looks around and then sits down. She waits with a slight show of impatience. There is a pause. Ford enters very confidently.**)

FORD   Greetings earthling. I may be a little late but I'm well worth waiting for. What! No grass skirt! I thought all you primitives wore grass skirts. Well, never mind, because I've forgotten to bring my lawnmower – still I'm sure we'll think of something. *(Pause)* And how shall we spend these precious moments together? A little food, a little wine, some soft music and...who knows...back to your place for you to slip into something comfortable? Or maybe a trip to the woods in my dumper truck, that transport of delights. *(Primrose is very carefully ignoring him. He pauses for a moment and then decides to try again.)* Hey, did I ever tell you what beautiful eyes you've got? Sultry and smouldering with a deep primitive passion.

PRIMROSE   *(She gives him a cold hard stare.)* Do you have to practise at being a moron or does it just come naturally? Perhaps you should slip into something comfortable – like a cesspit! I hope the disease you've got isn't catching, but then I don't think premature senility is, is it? *(She smiles very sweetly at Ford.)* Just so we know where we stand.

FORD   I think I get the message.

PRIMROSE   Good.

FORD   You must think I'm a perfect idiot.

PRIMROSE   Nobody's perfect. You think I'm an idiot though.

FORD   I could be wrong.

PRIMROSE   You could indeed.

FORD   I asked for that little lot, didn't I?

PRIMROSE   Every single word.

FORD   *(Pause)* Tell me something, what do you really think about us?

PRIMROSE   You mean, what do I think about you, don't you? You want to be careful, your slip's showing.

FORD   You leave my underwear out of this.

PRIMROSE   You show me yours and I'll show you mine.

FORD   OK.

PRIMROSE   I don't think you're as dumb as you make out.

FORD   Flattery will get you everywhere.

PRIMROSE   It's your eyes you see, it's the way they smoulder with a deep primitive passion.

FORD   You're alright, aren't you.

PRIMROSE   Your turn for compliments is it? *(Pause)* What did you expect when you arranged to meet me here?

FORD   I didn't expect you to bite back.

PRIMROSE   Us primitives sharpen our teeth. Didn't you know that?

FORD   So I've noticed. *(Pause)* I didn't know what to expect.

PRIMROSE   Come off it – you knew perfectly well what you were expecting.

FORD   I'm no romantic, that's something you ought to know.

When they were handing out the rose-coloured glasses they missed me out.

PRIMROSE Well at least that's two things we have in common.

FORD Two?

PRIMROSE I like you Ford and I think if you were to work really hard you could get to like me – on a good day, when the wind is in the right direction. I'm not an optimist about these things.

FORD *(Ford's mood suddenly appears to change – he becomes more serious.)* What are you going to do about the road?

PRIMROSE What do you suggest I do?

FORD You can leave with me if you like.

PRIMROSE Is that a proposition?

FORD It's anything you want, only don't stay here.

PRIMROSE Why not?

FORD Just don't that's all.

PRIMROSE The truth Ford!

FORD The truth is... *(He becomes flippant again)* ...I only show my slip on Mondays and today's Friday. I'm afraid you'll have to stick with me if you want the truth. *(Pause)* Come on, let's go for a walk.

PRIMROSE Perhaps we could go for a spin in your dumper truck. We could park up and slip onto the back seat.

FORD *(He laughs.)* It doesn't have a back seat. Anyway, who told you about that?

PRIMROSE Us girls stick together, you should know that.

FORD No I think we'll give the dumper truck a miss. A little walk will be enough.

PRIMROSE For now.

(PRIMROSE and FORD exit.)

JUNIPER	There's a turn-up for the book.
HYACINTH	We all know which side she's on.
ALTHEA	Meanwhile, back in the jungle things are stirring.

SCENE 4

(BRYONY **and** MARIGOLD **enter. They are carrying long sticks and knives with which to make spears.**)

MARIGOLD	'Let the wood of the forest defend the forest' – great! 'Make a spear,' he said. What he didn't say was how. I suppose if we sharpened the end of a stick it would do.
BRYONY	It wouldn't be very sharp, would it?
MARIGOLD	We could always hit them over the head with it.
BRYONY	Listen, if I was to bind my knife to the end of this stick it ought to make a pretty nasty spear, especially if the blade was really sharp. *(She starts to make a spear.)* What do you think?
MARIGOLD	It sounds pretty unpleasant to me.
BRYONY	That's the whole idea.
MARIGOLD	Could you really attack them – even hurt them?
BRYONY	Yes, if I have to. This is a fight we can't afford to lose.
MARIGOLD	I don't think I could.
BRYONY	Then what are you doing here?
MARIGOLD	It seemed like a good idea at the time – I think. Or maybe I'm just easily led. To tell you the truth I don't really know what I am doing here. Besides, I don't think I'd be much good in a fight.
BRYONY	Then you'll just have to stay out of the way won't you.
MARIGOLD	Perhaps I'll hide when the time comes.

(MOSS **enters.**)

MOSS   How are you getting on?

BRYONY   Alright.

MOSS   *(He sees the nearly finished spear.)* Hey, that's good.

BRYONY   It is, isn't it?

MARIGOLD   Moss?

MOSS   What?

MARIGOLD   Do you think we're really going to have to fight them?

MOSS   I have no doubts on that score.

MARIGOLD   Oh dear. *(She looks worried.)*

(ALDER, CLEOME **and** POPPY **enter.**)

CLEOME   We want to talk to you.

MOSS   Talk! That's all you're good for.

POPPY   We want to save the Tree as much as you do.

MOSS   Then why don't you join us?

POPPY   We don't have to fight. We can use ourselves to protect the Tree.

ALDER   We'll tie ourselves to it if we have to.

MOSS   Some good that'll do. If you ask me you'd be better hanging from the branches – by your necks.

ALDER   They'll have to kill us before we'll move.

MOSS   How do you know they won't?

ALDER   I don't believe they're that ruthless – it is only a road.

BRYONY   I wish I had your faith. *(She looks at the completed spear.)* There – finished. A little rough maybe, but it will serve its purpose well enough.

MARIGOLD   You couldn't make one for me could you?

BRYONY   I thought you were going to hide.

MARIGOLD   Well I might...but then again...

POPPY   You've not been listening to a word we've been saying.

BRYONY   Yes I have and I hope you succeed.

POPPY   Then why don't you join us?

BRYONY   If I thought it would work I would, but it won't do any good at all.

CLEOME   *(To Marigold)* What about you?

MARIGOLD   I'm with them – I think. Sorry.

CLEOME   But it's wrong.

BRYONY   Of course it is but maybe violence is justified if all else fails.

CLEOME   But everything else hasn't failed.

BRYONY   It will and in the meantime we've got to prepare.

(They all exit.)

AMARYLLIS The village burbles with activity.

HYACINTH   People scurrying hither and thither.

ALTHEA   Things to do, preparations to make.

JUNIPER   With joy in their hearts and a spring in their step they...flex their muscles.

SCENE 5

(RILEY and COLUMBINE **enter.)**

RILEY   Which side are you on?

COLUMBINE I don't know.

RILEY   Whatever happens you mustn't lose the tree.

COLUMBINE   Are you telling me that you believe in it?

RILEY   No, but I believe it's important to you and that you ought to do all you can to save it. It sort of represents everything that's good about the unspoilt existence you live here.

COLUMBINE   Unspoilt existence, eh?

RILEY   Yes – you have peace and contentment here. It's like paradise.

COLUMBINE   You see me as some kind of innocent don't you?

RILEY   I suppose I do, yes.

COLUMBINE   Is that why you've never suggested we make love?

RILEY   What!

COLUMBINE   I've given you enough opportunity. Don't you like me?

RILEY   Of course I do. *(Pause)* I think you're terrific if you really want to know. I just – didn't want to spoil anything.

COLUMBINE   Like my unspoilt existence, you mean.

RILEY   Something like that – yes.

COLUMBINE   Pity. *(Pause)* Let me tell you something – the Tree's going to be cut down, I know it is, and when that happens the world's going to end. But I'm not going to worry about it because it'll happen whether I worry or not. But I know what I'd rather be doing when it does happen. And it would be a shame to miss any more opportunities wouldn't it?

RILEY   Yes it would. *(Pause)* Columbine?

COLUMBINE   Yes?

RILEY   Do you think you could show me round the forest again?

COLUMBINE   I'd like that.

RILEY   Only I don't think we'll bother with the animals and the plants this time.

(COLUMBINE **and** RILEY **exit.**)

HYACINTH   An affair of the heart?

ALTHEA   Smut, smut, smut.

AMARYLLIS   Love's a wonderful thing, don't you agree?

ALTHEA   Smut, smut, smut.

SCENE 6

(SCOTT **enters and walks up to the** CHORUS **and** ASPEN.)

SCOTT   I was wondering if you'd looked at the photographs I gave you.

JUNIPER   Oh yes.

HYACINTH   We've studied them very carefully.

ALTHEA   Learned them off by heart, no less.

AMARYLLIS   They were fascinating.

SCOTT   Oh good, I'm glad you found them interesting. I've got some more pictures here if you'd like them. *(She gets some pictures out of her handbag and offers them to the Chorus – they ignore her.)*

ASPEN   Tell me, how do you like your job?

SCOTT   It's fine.

ASPEN   Really?

SCOTT   Well there are a few problems. It isn't easy working for the company – it isn't easy at all. It's so hard to stay true to one's self and be part of it all but I feel that the best way to change the system is to change it from the inside. Mind you sometimes I get fed up with it all. Sometimes I think I should pack it all in and do something useful – like being a social worker. I really feel I've got something to offer the unemployed. You see it isn't easy with a sociology degree. Ned, he's my live-in-feller, he's a freelance architect, he reckons I'm wasted. He thinks I should get a research post at a university. He feels that I've got a lot to contribute. I mean, just looking around here, there's so much of interest – it would make a terrific thesis. I really think I should draft a proposal just as soon as I get back to town.

JUNIPER   We think it's a superb idea.

SCOTT   You do?

HYACINTH   We'd make excellent specimens for study.

ALTHEA   And we'd be so co-operative.

AMARYLLIS   Tell me – do you know any good jokes?

(**The** CHORUS **turn away from** SCOTT. **Scott looks a little bemused, hesitates for a moment and then exits.**)

SCENE 7

(PRIMROSE **and** TANSY **enter. They have come to meet** FORD. MOSS **enters from the opposite side; he is carrying a spear.**)

MOSS   What do you want?

TANSY   Nothing.

MOSS   You're not welcome here.

TANSY   We've as much right to be here as you.

MOSS   You don't belong with us anymore, you belong with them.

PRIMROSE   So what!

MOSS   I'd stay with them if I were you – it might be safer.

TANSY   Threats, eh? You're just a big kid playing games. I only hope you realise it before you hurt yourself.

MOSS   Why don't you shut your face!

PRIMROSE   And why don't you leave us alone!

MOSS   You can keep your trap shut as well. We all know about you, don't we? I know what you get up to with Ford. Share you around do they?

PRIMROSE   How dare you!

TANSY   Listen foul mouth, when it's all over and that piece of wood over there *(She means the Tree.)* is lying on the ground and you're stood about with your spear dangling in your hand I shall be the first one to laugh.

MOSS   I'll show you! *(He raises his spear and starts to advance towards Tansy.)*

TANSY   You – you're all mouth.

MOSS   Is that so! *(He continues to advance with his spear at the ready.)* If there's going to be trouble maybe it should start here and now. Perhaps I should get rid of you first before we start on them. All mouth am I? We'll see about that!

(Moss moves to strike at Tansy; she backs away.)

(BRACT enters.)

BRACT   Stop it! *(Moss turns to look at Bract.)* What are you doing?

MOSS   I'm dealing with a traitor, that's what!

BRACT   You're a fool! If we have to kill anyone let it be the road builders – we are not going to start on our own people. It's bad enough what we're doing. For all our sakes, keep yourselves under control!

(FORD enters. He sizes up the situation very quickly. He puts himself between MOSS and the two girls.)

FORD   Greetings girls, been waiting long?

BRACT   You! Ford! I've got a message for your friends – if any of you try to harm the Tree we will kill all of you. And you had better believe me!

FORD   Oh I do, I do.

BRACT   *(To Moss)* Come on!

(BRACT and MOSS exit.)

FORD   My my, he is in a mood, isn't he? Looks like you'd better stick with me girls – things have definitely taken a downturn.

(FORD, PRIMROSE and TANSY exit.)

ALTHEA   The beetles are burrowing.

HYACINTH   The termites are eating the roots.

AMARYLLIS   You think so?

ALTHEA   Oh yes.

SCENE 8

(HOLLY runs in, followed by ASH.)

ASH   Come back!

HOLLY   Leave me alone!

ASH   Please!

HOLLY   No.

ASH   We've got to talk.

HOLLY   What is there to talk about? You've made your choice, now let me make mine. *(Pause)* Everything was fine – why did you have to go and spoil it?

ASH   You're the one who wants to leave, remember?

HOLLY   So did you.

ASH   I just wanted to be with you.

HOLLY   Then why are you doing it? There was a time when you didn't give a damn about the Tree. You were always half-asleep.

ASH   Maybe I've woken up.

HOLLY   Why are you doing it?

ASH   I'm doing it for you.

HOLLY   That's stupid, I don't want you to bother. I want us to leave together, that's what I want.

ASH   I can't.

HOLLY   Why not?

ASH   Because I'm frightened.

HOLLY   Of what?

ASH   If they cut the Tree down it'll mean the end of everything. I can't understand what 'everything' means – the only thing I know is that it would be the end of you. *(Pause)* Of you and me. What right have they to stop us before we've even begun! We didn't ask for the road! *(Pause)* You know how I feel about you, don't you?

HOLLY   Yes. *(Pause)* You can still come with me when it's all over.

ASH   No I can't. Even if we win this time they'll try again.

HOLLY   I've got to leave – you must understand that.

ASH   Yes, I know.

(ASH looks at HOLLY and then he walks out. SORREL, ALLYSSUM and TANSY enter.)

ASPEN   So you're leaving too?

SORREL   Yes, it seems like a good time.

ASPEN   It won't be easy.

ALLYSSUM   I don't suppose it was easy being born but it was worth it.

SORREL   It's unnatural that we should be hemmed in by the forest – there are too many limits.

HOLLY   For some of us it isn't enough to rehearse for old age.

TANSY   The truth is – we want out!

ASPEN   The road lies that way.

TANSY   And we're going to take it.

HYACINTH   But what happens when the Tree is cut down?

SORREL   The Tree stands for everything that is wrong here. As long as we believed we were held fast, its branches gripping us, its roots fixing us to the spot. We're free of it now; we can leave.

AMARYLLIS   Have a good journey.

TANSY   It may not be good but at least it'll be interesting.

ALTHEA   The others are going to fight.

ALLYSSUM   We know. It gives us no pleasure to leave a divided community. We were once all friends.

SORREL   Come on, let's go.

(SORREL, ALLYSSUM, TANSY **and** HOLLY **exit.**)

SCENE 9

JUNIPER   Watch now.

HYACINTH   Watch carefully. Things are coming to a head.

AMARYLLIS   And the joke?

ALTHEA   It's the way they're told, did you not know that?

AMARYLLIS   And how is this joke to be told?

JUNIPER   Like I said – watch now.

HYACINTH Watch carefully and look out for the punchline.

    (FORD, MORRIS and PRIMROSE enter.)

ALTHEA Hello, here they come. We're off. I think we'd better take our seats.

FORD Well it's still here. *(He looks across at the dumper truck.)* I'd have expected them to have smashed it up or at the very least written ROAD BUILDERS GO HOME all over it. *(He beats on a mudguard.)* Listen! Jungle drums! The natives are restless tonight!

MORRIS Do you think things will get really nasty?

FORD I hope that's a wig you're wearing. They say that scalping could come back into fashion in a big way. *(To Primrose)* Hey sunshine, do they go in for that sort of thing around here?

PRIMROSE Not usually, though I daresay they might make an exception in your case.

FORD That's what I like to hear – words of love.

MORRIS Everything was going so well before Allard turned up. Where is she, by the way?

FORD The last time I saw her she was parading around exposing her tape measure to the world. She seemed to be going round in ever decreasing circles and I am confident that she will eventually disappear, closely followed up the same orifice by the others.

MORRIS You know what, I reckon God's got a sense of humour. *(He has been staring at the Tree.)*

FORD What?

MORRIS It would be just like God, wouldn't it, to put a tree right in the middle of nowhere and then rest the sky on it? It's such a daft idea that it might even be true. Then we'd come along. We'd be lulled by a false sense of security because we always believe we're right. We wouldn't recognise the end of the world if it fell on us.

We'd only have to make the wrong decision once. This could be it. I can just imagine the looks on our faces when the sky fell on us. I reckon God would laugh himself silly. Have you noticed what an amazing coincidence it is that this particular tree just happens to be exactly in the path of the road.

FORD   Do you really believe that?

MORRIS   No, but it's something else to worry about, isn't it?

(Enter ALLARD, SCOTT, AUSTIN and BENTLEY.)

SCOTT   I warned you what would happen. You've managed to create an incident out of nothing.

ALLARD   Look, when that tree comes crashing down and they see that everything is OK, then they'll shut up. *(To Austin)* Right then, there's the tree, how do you propose to cut it down?

AUSTIN   If it was up to me I'd leave it where it is. I'm sure the company wouldn't mind a little detour.

FORD   It would make a nice centre-piece for a service station. You could call it the 'Tree Services' – they've all got to have a name, it would be a real attraction.

ALLARD   Shut up! It's coming down. Have you got a chainsaw?

FORD   *(He pats his pockets.)* Chainsaw...chainsaw...no, sorry!

AUSTIN   We didn't bring one, the last thing we expected was to be chopping down trees.

ALLARD   At least you must have an axe.

MORRIS   Who'd be fool enough to stand there chopping down the tree while a bunch of wild natives are busy chopping us down? They're making spears, did you know that?

AUSTIN   It doesn't matter anyway because we don't have an axe.

FORD   *(To Primrose)* I don't suppose your people would lend us one? *(Primrose shakes her head.)* No, I thought not.

MORRIS   Well there we are then, we'll just have to forget the whole idea and leave the tree where it is. Oh dear, what a pity.

BENTLEY   Dynamite!

MORRIS   Yes it is a good idea, isn't it?

BENTLEY   We could use dynamite to blow up the tree. It's quick and it's simple.

ALLARD   Have we got any?

BENTLEY   Yes – I've got some in my bag with the seismic testing-kit. It won't take much to blow up the tree. I've even got a battery to detonate it.

FORD   Aren't you the little boy scout!

ALLARD   That settles it. Quite an apt solution, really. In one swift act they'll see for themselves what civilisation can do.

SCOTT   Do we have to go trampling over their culture any more than necessary? They have a right to their place in history.

ALLARD   This little lot were forgotten before they even existed and they didn't exist until we found them. When it's all written down they won't even merit a mention on the fashion page. *(She stops and looks around.)* Where's Riley?

AUSTIN   I don't know.

SCOTT   The last time I saw him he was with one of the girls.

ALLARD   We'd better find him. I don't want anything to happen to him – that would really slow things down. You three stay here and set things up. *(To Scott)* Come on, we'll go and look for him.

(ALLARD and SCOTT exit.)

BENTLEY   Right, we'd better get on with it. Hold this, will you? *(He gives the dynamite to Austin.)*

AUSTIN   Are you sure this will be enough?

BENTLEY   More than enough for what we have to do. If you tape
it to the tree I'll run the wire and set up the detonating
switch. *(He gives Austin some tape and they begin to set up the
dynamite.)*

FORD   You know it's very nice watching other people work.

AUSTIN   You could always lend a hand.

FORD   I could, couldn't I? *(He does not move but continues to look at
Austin.)*

AUSTIN   Then why don't you?

FORD   I don't really think we should be doing this. After
what we're going to do to the poor sods, the least we
could do is to leave them their tree.

PRIMROSE   What do you mean? The truth Ford!

FORD   Are you old enough to hear it?

PRIMROSE   Don't be stupid!

FORD   I've seen it all before, you see – more times than I care
to remember. Peaceful communities minding their own
business and then we'd come along with our roads and
our chainsaws and our factory farms. In five years' time
all this will be gone and your people will be begging
by the side of the road. Prostitution will be a growth
industry – you don't need much in the way of
qualifications for that; I think they call it a service
industry. And don't think that those who leave will
fare much better either. The city slums will suck them
in and the sweat shops will fling open their doors. And
in ten years' time the forest will have disappeared and
the soil will have blown away and then those farms
will move on to pastures new leaving this place as an
empty sterile desert. That, my love, is the truth.

PRIMROSE   What about me?

FORD   Stick with me and you'll be alright. I'll give you a crash-course in how to survive.

PRIMROSE   And the others?

FORD   Them – they are down the chute!

PRIMROSE   I should tell them. They have a right to know.

FORD   You can do what you like but it won't do any good.

PRIMROSE   But you're part of it – you're a road builder too.

FORD   We're all road builders. I'd be part of it if I was sitting in my armchair a thousand miles from here.

PRIMROSE   Why don't you do something about it?

FORD   What is it they say? 'I was just obeying orders' and 'If it wasn't me it would be someone else'.

PRIMROSE   Stop it! If you want me to stay with you I want the truth.

FORD   I know what I should do but like everyone else I'm swept along on a tide of events outside my control. I can't do anything, I'm just one person. I can look after me – just about. We could look after each other. But don't expect anything more than that – anything else is just window-dressing.

AUSTIN   You're a hypocrite Ford – a bloody hypocrite. You were as keen as any of us to tell them the good news.

FORD   Stay with me. *(He ignores Bentley and looks at Primrose.)*

PRIMROSE   OK.

AUSTIN   Sod you, Ford.

(Enter BRACT, MOSS, BRYONY, MARIGOLD and ASH. **They are all carrying spears.)**

FORD   Hello – it looks like things are going to get very interesting.

MORRIS   I knew they'd be hostile – I was right all along.

FORD   Now is not the time to gloat.

(AUSTIN **picks up a piece of wood to use as a club. He gives it to** BENTLEY.)

AUSTIN   Here, take this. *(He picks up another one for himself.)*

BRACT   What's all this?! *(He indicates the dynamite that is taped to the Tree.)*

AUSTIN   It's none of your business.

(BRACT **and the rest stand, spears at the ready, in front of** AUSTIN **and** BENTLEY **who have their clubs in their hands. A fight looks imminent.**)

FORD   *(He whispers to Morris.)* It's like the gunfight at the OK Corral.

BRYONY   Why have you fastened this to the Tree? *(She indicates the dynamite.)*

AUSTIN   I've told you, it's none of your business.

BRACT   *(To Bryony)* Remove it!

BENTLEY   Leave it alone!

BRACT   How are you going to stop us?

BENTLEY   Oh, we'll do our best.

FORD   *(Quietly to Morris)* Come on – the Lone Ranger and Tonto to the rescue.

MORRIS   I hope you know what you're doing – Kemo Saby.

(They start to edge behind Austin and Bentley.)

BRYONY   It's something to hurt the Tree. I know it!

(BRYONY **goes to the dynamite to tear it off the Tree.** BENTLEY **steps in front of her,** AUSTIN **joins him.**)

BENTLEY   I said 'leave it'.

BRYONY   What if I don't?

BENTLEY   If it's a fight you want we'll give you one. Come on! Who's going to be first?

FORD   Me!

BENTLEY   What are you doing?!

(FORD **disarms** BENTLEY **and pushes him to the ground.** MORRIS **leaps on** AUSTIN **but has trouble getting the club off him.**)

AUSTIN   Morris! Are you crazy?

(MORRIS **and** AUSTIN **struggle. Morris is thrown to the ground.**)

MORRIS   Come on somebody! Give me a hand.

BRACT   Come on!

(BRACT **and the rest rush forward and surround** AUSTIN. **They level their spears at him.**)

BRACT   That's enough. Now!

(AUSTIN **gives up.**)

BENTLEY   Why Ford?

FORD   I told you.

PRIMROSE   *(To Ford)* Thank you.

MORRIS   Yeh – thanks. *(He picks himself up.)*

FORD   That, by the way, is something called dynamite.

BENTLEY   Shut up!

FORD   It is, as you so astutely surmised, there to bring down the tree.

MOSS   Smash it!

FORD   I wouldn't if I were you it might prove a little unhealthy. *(He walks over to the dynamite.)* Look, all you have to do is to remove these two little wires and the whole thing is rendered totally harmless. *(He pulls out the wires.)* See?

BRYONY   We didn't ask for your help. We could have managed on our own.

FORD   Hello, it's little miss sunshine.

BENTLEY   *(To Bryony)* I tell you now, you wouldn't have got far.

BRACT   You! Keep quiet!

BRYONY   What are we going to do now? The others may return at any minute.

MOSS   Kill them! It will be two less to deal with.

BRYONY   Moss is right. If we make an example of these two the rest will know where we stand.

FORD   If you kill them or any of us for that matter then more people will come and they will kill you. There are lots of us out there and we have weapons the like of which you can't even imagine. Then they'd cut your tree down anyway.

MOSS   We don't care – we'll kill all of you if we have to.

FORD   I don't doubt that for one minute. You've got plenty of bravado, what you need is a bit more brains. If I were you I'd keep them as hostages – even Allard won't risk their lives. You can hold them as long as necessary. She can't stop the road so she'll have to build round the tree and then you'll have got what you wanted and nobody will have got hurt.

BRYONY   He's lying. It could be some sort of trick.

FORD   I know, white man speak with fork tongue.

BRYONY   What?

FORD   I've just helped you, haven't I?

BRACT   Whose side are you on?

FORD   Mine. *(Pause)* Well?

MOSS   I say kill them now!

BRACT   No, Ford's right, it's the best chance we've got.

(Enter CLEOME, POPPY **and** ALDER. **They see that the others have their spears levelled at** AUSTIN **and** BENTLEY.**)**

CLEOME   Stop! Leave them alone!

MARIGOLD   It's alright, we're not going to do anything.

MOSS   Not yet, anyway.

POPPY   We were afraid we might be too late.

BRACT   We're going to keep them as hostages.

ALDER   What about them? *(He indicates Ford and Morris.)*

BRYONY   They helped us – much to our amazement.

CLEOME   We came here to save the Tree.

POPPY   Maybe between us we can do something.

ALDER   They'll have to kill us first if they try to destroy it.

CLEOME   Come on, let's do it.

(CLEOME, POPPY **and** ALDER **gather round the Tree.)**

POPPY   They can't ignore us now, can they?

(Pause)

BRACT   Now what?

CLEOME   We wait until Allard gets here.

FORD   *(Pause)* Anybody got a pack of cards? *Monopoly* set? *(He starts to hum the theme from 'High Noon'.)*

MORRIS   Be quiet.

FORD   *(Pause)* Anybody know any good jokes?

BRYONY   Why do you find everything so amusing? Don't you ever take anything seriously?

FORD   It's just my natural sunny personality shining through the gloom.

BRYONY   Well I wish you'd give it a rest.

BRACT   *(To the Chorus)* Made up your minds yet?

JUNIPER   Not exactly.

HYACINTH   The most realistic course of action is to do nothing, to bury our heads in the sand and hope it goes away.

AMARYLLIS Maybe it will.

ALTHEA   Then again.

JUNIPER   But in the meantime we don't want to miss the fun.

(Enter SORREL, ALLYSSUM, TANSY **and** HOLLY.**)**

MOSS   You lot can clear off. You're not wanted here.

ALLYSSUM   We've come to help if we can.

POPPY   Why should you – you don't believe.

ALLYSSUM   We did once.

MOSS   We don't want your help!

TANSY   See – I told you it would be a waste of time.

(Enter ALLARD, SCOTT, RILEY **and** COLUMBINE.**)**

ALLARD   Alright, what's going on here?

BRACT   Stay back or we kill them! *(He puts his spear up to Bentley's throat.)*

BENTLEY   It's all Ford's fault – he helped them.

ALLARD   You're finished Ford.

FORD   It is a far, far better thing...et cetera...et cetera...et cetera.

ALLARD   You've had your fun and games, now let them go.

MOSS   We mean it!

AUSTIN   They're not joking.

ALLARD   Neither am I.

ASH   We don't want to hurt them unless we have to. Promise you'll leave the Tree alone and we'll let them go.

ALLARD   If I promised that I'd be lying and you wouldn't believe me anyway. No, face facts, they have to be released and that tree has to go.

ASH   We can hold them forever if we have to. You can't make us release them.

ALLARD   Can't I?

(ALLARD **reaches into her handbag and takes out the revolver. The** PEOPLE, **who have never seen a gun before, do not react.**)

FORD   Oh Christ, I didn't bargain for that.

ALLARD   Now, let them go!

FORD   The game's over. Nice try. I'd do as she says if I were you.

ASH   Why should we?

ALLARD   Oh I see. Well let me explain something – this is a gun. It is a weapon capable of killing you where you stand. So I'm warning you, let them go!

ASH   No, I'm warning you. *(He begins to advance towards Allard.)* Why don't you go away and leave us in peace. We didn't ask for you to come.

ALLARD   Keep back!

ASH   *(He is still advancing with his spear at the ready.)* We ought to let you kill the Tree: it would serve you right, but we can't. It isn't them who deserve to die *(He indicates Austin and Bentley.)* – it's you! If we get rid of you maybe things will be alright. *(He moves closer.)*

ALLARD   Don't! It isn't worth it. It will all be over in a few minutes and then you can get on with your lives.

ASH   No!

ALLARD   Don't make me!

ASH   I don't care.

(ASH **lunges at** ALLARD. **She fires. Ash drops to the ground.**)

HOLLY   Ash!

(MOSS **rushes to kill** BENTLEY. ALLARD **points the gun at him.**)

ALLARD   Don't bother!

(MOSS **stops.**)

ALLARD   All of you, put your spears down! **(They do so.)**

RILEY   You didn't have to kill him.

ALLARD   They have to learn, Riley, they have to learn.

JUNIPER   You heard – we have to learn.

HYACINTH   It's a hard lesson. Re-adjust your mind, that's the . custom.

ALLARD   It will save lives in the long run, you see. *(Pause)* The sooner we're finished with this business the better. Is the dynamite OK?

BENTLEY   Ford disconnected it but it's all there.

ALLARD   Connect it up. *(Bentley goes to connect up the charge.)* Those of you round the tree had better move or you'll get hurt.

CLEOME   No! We've pledged to defend the Tree with our bodies.

ALLARD   Have you people no sense? I don't want to hurt you, I just want to do my job. Isn't one death enough? What you are doing isn't worth it.

CLEOME   Nevertheless we intend to stay.

ALLARD   Alright then, if that's what you want, that's what you'll get. *(To Austin)* Blow it up!

AUSTIN   I can't, not with all those people.

ALLARD   Then I will. *(She moves to the detonating switch.)*

FORD   Hang on a minute, let me talk to them.

ALLARD   Alright.

FORD   Listen, if she presses the button the dynamite will explode and the tree will come crashing down. You will be killed or injured. She'll do it whether you're there or not. You tell us that you like to think things over – so think about this. If the sky really does fall down then it won't matter whether you're blown up or not. But what happens if we are still here when the tree has fallen and the dust has settled? You will have made a gesture for nothing. Isn't it always better to compromise, to hedge your bets even a little? Are you so certain? Is there not even a one per cent doubt and isn't that one per cent worth counting? It is a matter of absolute certainty that the tree is going to come down. You know it and I know it. Be realistic. Don't make empty gestures.

JUNIPER   You may as well watch the end of the world from over here.

HYACINTH You'll get a much better view.

BRACT   It's over. Finished. We've lost. *(He looks at the others.)* You must make up your own minds.

           (CLEOME walks slowly away from the Tree. The others look at each other and then they too walk away.)

FORD   It's all yours.

ALLARD   I shall be glad to see the end of this.

FORD   You could always forget it and let them keep their tree.

ALLARD   No I couldn't. It's going. Now!

           (ALLARD raises her hand to detonate the charge.)

ASPEN   Stop! *(Everyone turns to look at her.)* You have come to a fork in the road. Before you rush headlong down one of the paths it is ever prudent to contemplate possible destinations. If we are right and you destroy the Tree then the sky will fall and eternal darkness will be upon us. If you are right and you destroy the Tree it will still be the end of everything. For us you will have destroyed our identity but for you also it will mean oblivion. Not swiftly with the fall of this particular tree but slowly and with inevitable stealth. For as you rip the heart out of the great forest, as you surely will, so the sky will drop gently and ever softly to smother us all. Each tree taken diminishes the whole and drains away the lifeblood of the earth.

FORD   *(He looks at Allard.)* Well?

ALLARD   I've had enough of this. I've got a job to do.

AMARYLLIS   Watch their faces when the end comes.

ALTHEA   The joke will be worth the telling.

ALLARD   Now!

(ALLARD **pushes the button which detonates the charge – it explodes. Everyone watches as the Tree slowly falls to the ground. In silence the CREW start to clear up and the PEOPLE begin to leave slowly. PRIMROSE and FORD stand together, watching. ASPEN and the CHORUS are also watching. Aspen begins to smile, and then, very softly at first and then louder, the Chorus begin to laugh. A low rolling sound is heard which gets louder and louder. Everyone looks up. Allard and the Crew look puzzled; they don't realise what is happening. Ford does and he begins to smile. As the sound mounts to a crescendo the lights begin to dim. The Chorus are still laughing. Some of the People begin to scream. Allard and the Crew suddenly realise what they've done, the Chorus see the realisation, and they laugh with renewed vigour. We see all the cast being pressed to the ground. The sky falls on them.**

Blackout. Silence.)

The End

THE MAKING OF THE PLAY

When I was approached by the Hampshire County Youth Theatre to write a play for them, this was the one I wanted to write. I was asked to write for a cast of twenty-six young people who were going to spend three weeks in residence, rehearsing and then performing for three nights. One of the parameters I set myself was that every actor should have an interesting and worthwhile part.

Before I took up writing seriously I thought (if I thought about it at all) that writers simply sat down at a typewriter and began at the beginning and carried on until they got to the end and then they stopped. When they stopped, there was the finished piece of work hot off the typewriter. I now know differently – there is something called rewriting. Let me explain how this play was written. The first thing I did was to produce a very rough hand-written version. I then scribbled notes all over it and rewrote the play to produce a second 'very rough hand-written version'. I then wrote notes all over this version and used it to produce a type-written version – this was the official first draft. I gave this to the director to find out what he thought about it. I also had a number of new ideas that I wanted to include so I rewrote the play yet again to produce a second type-written draft. This was the version that we used to begin rehearsals. During rehearsals there was a great deal more discussion between the director, the cast and myself. Yet more rewriting was required as it became apparent that some things worked better than others and that the play needed additional scenes. Eventually I got a version that I liked and that seemed to work and this was the one that the audience saw. There was yet more rewriting for this, the published version.

Paul King.

FOLLOW-UP ACTIVITIES

Casting the play

One of the earliest tasks in producing a performance of a play is casting. At the beginning of this script, the playwright has provided a cast list with quite detailed descriptions of the characters. For example:

Austin   The foreman. He will usually get the job done without asking too many questions unless it really goes against the grain.

There are also clues about the characters in the script, shown by the things said or done by a character, and by other characters' reactions to him or her.

Choose a couple of characters and write down some ideas about their personalities. What things help characterisation? Behaviour, appearance, dress, accent, class?

Compare your ideas with those of the person next to you. How much do you agree with one another? Discuss your differences of opinion.

'We don't care – we'll kill all of you if we have to' (p. 68). Scene from the original production of The Tree that holds up the Sky, *1985* (Photograph by Glenn Collett).

Designing the play

No two productions of a play script are ever the same. Each has its own style, its own look, its own interpretation. A number of different technical and artistic activities (e.g. lighting, sound, acting, set and costume) combine to give a total effect. In designing the set, for example, the designer must bear in mind the intentions of the play, that the set has to be practical for actors to work on and interesting for an audience to look at. It also has to be built of materials that can be afforded or borrowed easily.

When the play was first performed it was staged in a large circus tent. The audience was seated on three sides. On the fourth side a scaffolding was built for the band and the Chorus. The Tree was placed centrally in the acting area and was made of light plastic drain piping. No attempt was made to disguise the drain pipe – it was felt that a symbolic tree would suit the style of the play. Being plastic and very light, when it was felled at the end of the play, it did not do any damage.

What ideas do you have for designing the set and/or costumes? Draw plans or sketches. Make lists of materials (texture), colours etc. that you might use.

What space are you going to perform in? Will it be a 'picture-frame stage' *(proscenium arch)* with the audience separated from the stage by an arch, or will it be performed with the audience surrounding the performers on all sides *(theatre-in-the-round)*? What differences will the choice make?

Look at the photograph on p. 76. Are these the sorts of costumes you had imagined?

Directing the play

No performance of a play is ever the work of just one person. The writer's ideas are worked on, expanded and changed by all the different people who work on the play – actors, set designers and set builders, lighting designers, lighting technicians, and the director. The director will probably start out with a picture in her or his head of how the production should look and sound. This will change in rehearsals and through the influence of those she or he works alongside. Other issues such as money, theatre space, technical facilities and the sort of audience which may see the play will also shape the final production.

Write some notes on how you as a director might decide to put the play together. Consider the following points:

- *Will it be interpreted as an historical piece or presented in a futuristic style?*
- *Will the actors be funny and lively or serious and thoughtful?*
- *What will the lighting bar/set be like? Will it use lots of colour and be obvious to the audience or be like a real forest with subtle areas of light and shade? Will there be a tree? Will the tree be real with a trunk and branches or just suggested? Will there be a dumper truck? Can you get it into your theatre or school hall? If not, will you have a replacement — noises off-stage or a mock-up made of set-building materials?*

Characterisation

As an actor, understanding the character you play is very important. What things in the script help understand the characters? Look at *Allard* as an example. What sort of person is she? Is she easily influenced by people around her?

What about *Ford?* What is his attitude to the 'locals'? Does it change during the play? Who influences him and how? Is he gentle and quiet; loud and understanding?

Write notes about both Allard **and** Ford **as characters. Imagine that you are going to give these notes to an actor. What do you need her or him to know?**

Design costumes for Allard **and Ford. You may like to look through old magazines for images that you think suit the characters. Think about how clothes reflect personalities. How does this aid you in making decisions about colour and texture as well as the actual garments?**

Drama ideas and improvisation

Actors often use improvisation as a way of exploring a script or understanding a character. What sort of improvisations can you design to help you achieve both these aims? Try them out with a friend or a group of friends.

Imagine you are a 'local' from the village. Tell your best friend how you first found out about the Tree. Get your best friend to tell you how she or he learnt about the Tree. Consider the following:

- *Did you believe all that you were told?*
- *Do you still celebrate 'Treeday'?*
- *If you still celebrate 'Treeday' is it simply out of habit or because it is an important experience in your life?*
- *What do you think 'Treeday' means to other people in the community?*

In a small group act out the memories of the best 'Treeday' you can remember.

In a small group act out meeting a surveyor or a survey team for the first time.

- *Have you seen outsiders before?*
- *Are you trusting, questioning or hostile?*
- *What are the attitudes of the surveyors?*

As a class or a large group arrange your own meeting to discuss the arrival of the survey team. Imagine what impressions the survey team has made on you and examine how this differs from those of your friends. What are you going to do? You may like to think of similar ideas that affect people's lives and find ways of exploring them through drama.

With a partner, imagine you are a surveyor about to set out on an expedition and tell your partner what it is you are leaving behind.

- *What will you miss most?*
- *What will you miss least?*
- *What do you expect to find?*
- *What do you fear?*

Imagine a small group of you are the sole survivors after the demolition of the Tree. Some of you are 'locals' and some of you are surveyors. Explore discovering yourself still alive and discovering the presence of other people. What are you going to do now? What are the strategies for survival?

Writing tasks

The playwright has described the process of writing this play earlier in this section. It was originally conceived as a musical and when it was considered for publication in the *Act Now* series he decided to rewrite it as an ordinary play. This meant changing some small scenes.

There were many reasons for the changes. Sometimes writers change their work because over time they have reconsidered how or what they have written. You often hear people saying that they liked a play, but if you asked them why they cannot explain other than to say 'I just did'.

Make a list of the things you like about the play and a list of the things you don't like. Having done this, write a short discussion on your overall impression using some of the ideas from the lists.

No ideas are totally original. We are all influenced by things we have seen, heard or experienced before. To write a play we need to know what a play is – we need to have seen one on stage. We need also to have seen a play set out on paper.

Write about where you think the playwright may have got his ideas.

Write about other plays, films or books with similar themes. How differently are they treated?

Write your own short play, poem, story or song prompted by having read *The Tree that holds up the Sky*.